T0149495

Spiritual Lessons for New Believers

Follow Up

Keith D. Pisani

WESTBOW
PRESS®
A DIVISION OF THOMAS NELSON
& ZONDERVAN

WestBow Press books may be ordered through booksellers or by contacting:

WestBow Press
A Division of Thomas Nelson & Zondervan
1663 Liberty Drive
Bloomington, IN 47403
www.westbowpress.com
1 (866) 928-1240

Scripture taken from the King James Version of the Bible
(https://www.biblegateway.com/versions/King-James-Version-KJV-Bible/#copy)

ISBN: 978-1-5127-7063-6 (sc)
ISBN: 978-1-5127-7062-9 (e)

Library of Congress Control Number: 2017900232

Print information available on the last page.

WestBow Press rev. date: 11/18/2019

Spiritual Lessons for New Believers
(Follow-Up Guide for New Believers)

Introduction

Training Notes for Disciplers

Your Faith in Christ

Your Life in Christ

Your Walk with Christ

Your Fellowship with Christ and His People

Answers to the Follow-Up Sessions

Transitional Study: (Baptism Class)

Transitional Study: (Membership Class)

Addendum: (How to Study the Bible)

Answers for How to Study the Bible

Follow-Up

Just as physical babies should not be left on the doorstep to fend for themselves, neither should spiritual babies be left to grow on their own. Paul's approach to discipleship was "as a nurse cherisheth her children: so being affectionately desirous of you, we were willing to have imparted unto you, not the gospel of God only, but also our own souls, because you were dear to us" (1 Thessalonians 1:6–7). The early church cared for new converts as a mother cares for her newborn baby. Should the modern church do less?

Follow-up is the initial phase of discipleship. Follow-up begins after a person receives Jesus Christ as Savior. The salvation experience may take place inside the church at an altar call, in a classroom, through a children's ministry, or during a harvest event. A person may come to Christ and experience regeneration outside the church during an outreach event, one-on-one, or group evangelism, with a believer, or apart from a believer in the privacy of a person's one-on-One time with God. Wherever salvation happens, Christians are responsible to initiate follow-up.

The purpose of follow-up is spiritual growth toward maturity in Jesus Christ.

The four-session *Spiritual Lessons for New Believers* is phase 1 of a new believer's follow-up studies. Phase 1 leads into two transitional studies: "Baptism Class" and "Membership Class." Phase 2 is the author's twenty-six-session *Spiritual Lessons for Growing Believers: A to Z* study with its companion workbook: *Spiritual Lessons for Growing Believers Workbook*.

Physical babies grow. Babies who do not grow are given special medical attention to promote physical growth. Just as a non growing physical baby is considered an aberration, it is considered not normal for a babe in Christ to remain spiritually immature. Just as first-century believers grew "in the grace and knowledge of our Lord and Savior Jesus Christ" (2 Peter 3:18), modern believers should grow into maturity for Jesus Christ.

When a person receives Jesus Christ as Savior, a believer who is trained in the four phase 1 follow-up sessions should take the first of those four sessions, give one copy to the new convert, and keep one copy as the presenter. The presenter (now called the discipler) will take the new convert, open the first session, and review the instructions on the top of the first study. "My name is _____ _____" is the name of the new convert being discipled. "My helper's name and phone number (contact information) is _____" is the name of the discipler. Both the new convert and the discipler will need a Bible for study and a writing instrument (like a pen or a pencil) to fill in the blanks and to take notes. The study is keyed to the 1611 King James Version of the Bible.

If both the discipler and the new convert are available, the first session can begin immediately in a private setting. Males follow up males. Females follow up females. Approved workers follow up children. (Those discipling children can elect to use the author's follow-up guide for children: *Jesus Loves Me: A Follow-Up Guide for Children*). The session is taught or led out loud by the discipler (Christ said, in Matthew 28:18–19, that teaching is an effective discipleship method.) If the first session begins immediately, the discipler and new convert can, at the end of session 1, arrange for a prescribed place, date, and time to meet for session 2. After session 2 is taught or led and completed, the discipler and new convert can establish a prescribed place, date, and time to meet for session 3. This same pattern of establishing a prescribed place, date, and time to meet is true for session 4.

Just after the new convert's salvation experience, if both the discipler and the new convert have a scheduling conflict and cannot begin immediately, the discipler should make an appointment with the new convert and establish a prescribed place, date, and time when both the discipler and the new convert can meet. If no time is available, the discipler can assign the first study as a take-home assignment to be brought back for review, with the discipler, at a prescribed place, date, and time. If this latter arrangement is made, the discipler will review the answers to session 1, make comments, and then lead or teach session

2 to the new convert. At the conclusion of session 2, the discipler can assign session 3 as a take-home assignment, ask the new convert to bring session 3 back for review, and then, after session 3 has been reviewed by the discipler, session 4 can be led or taught by the discipler. Once all four sessions have been completed, the new convert will be asked to enroll in two transition studies that lead to church membership: a one-session baptism class and a one-session membership class. These two transition studies are included in this book. Also, the author has included a session on "How to Study the Bible." All of these studies (the four-session follow-up studies, the two transitional studies, and the one-session study on "How to Study the Bible') are included in the author's next-step, twenty-six-lesson, phase 2 discipleship study: *Spiritual Lessons for Growing Believers: Bible Basics from A to Z.*[1]

In making disciples, we are not making disciples of ourselves. We are making disciples of Jesus Christ. It is a privilege to serve Jesus in making disciples of new converts, seeing them grow into maturity for Christ.

The four sessions include the reading content of instructive opening paragraphs, fill-in-the-blank questions, matching, some memorization, and some writing. The minimal qualifications needed to use the follow-up materials, as a

---

1 The twenty-six session *Spiritual Lessons for Growing Believers* study guide, along with its fill-in-the-blank companion workbook, *Spiritual Lessons for Growing Believers Workbook*, can be obtained through WestBow Press or through the author's website: www.keithpisaniministries.com. Additional follow-up studies for children (*Jesus Loves Me: A Follow-Up Guide for Children*) can be obtained the same way.

discipler, are the discipler must be a believer and the discipler must be able to read.

May God bless the use of these follow-up studies. They are cross-generational and adaptable to all age groups. My prayer is that all believers will grow into maturity for Christ.[2]

---

[2] All scripture quotations are from the 1611 King James Version of the Bible.

Follow-Up (1) Your Faith in Christ

My name is _____.

My helper's name and phone number is _____

_____.

Please read the following paragraph out loud:

The person who receives Jesus Christ as Savior is the recipient of many blessings. The believer is a new creation in Jesus Christ (2 Corinthians 5:17), becomes a citizen of heaven (Philippians 3:20), acquires a new inheritance (Ephesians 1:3–14), and is the beneficiary of many promises (John 14:1–3), and the believer's salvation is secure (John 10:28–30).

The purpose of this study is to review some blessings that accompany salvation. Read the scripture references given. Then place appropriate answers in the spaces provided.

1. How does God describe an unsaved person?

   The unsaved person is like a sheep which has gone _____ (Isaiah 53:6).

   The unsaved person is _____ already because he has not believed in Jesus Christ as Savior (John 3:18).

   The unsaved person has _____ _____ of the glory (righteous standards) of God   (Romans 3:23).

   The unsaved person will be cast into the _____ _____ _____ because his or her name is not found written in the book of life (Revelation 20:15).

2. How does God describe the saved person?

   The saved person is _____ _____ (John 3:3, 7). This phrase means "to be born from above (born from heaven)."

   The saved person is _____ _____ because he or she has believed in Jesus Christ as Savior (John 3:18).

   The saved person is a new _____ in Jesus Christ (2 Corinthians 5:17).

The saved person is a newborn _____ (1 Peter 2:2).

The saved person's sins are _____ because of Jesus Christ (1 John 2:12).

3. How long does salvation last?

   The person who believes in Jesus Christ knows he or she has _____ _____ (1 John 5:13).

   The person who has eternal life shall never _____ (John 10:28).

4. Who guarantees that salvation will last forever?

   The _____ Himself bears witness with our spirit that we are the _____ of God (Romans 8:16).

   The believer is kept (guaranteed salvation) by the power of _____ through faith unto salvation (1 Peter 1:5).

5. Read 1 John 5:12. Then answer the following question:

   Are you sure that you will enter heaven beyond this life? _____ Yes _____ Not Sure

6. Based on your understanding of the Bible, answer the following question:

   If you were to die today and meet God, and He should ask you why He should let you into His heaven, what would you say?

   _____

   _____

   _____

   _____

   _____

   _____

7. John 3:16 describes how God provided for humankind's salvation. Make this verse personal. Please place your name in the spaces provided.

   For God so loved _____, that He gave His only (uniquely) begotten Son (Jesus); that _____ who believes in Him should not perish but that _____ should have everlasting life. (John 3:16)

8. Review sections 1–7. Answer the following questions:

   Have you received Jesus Christ as your personal Lord and Savior? _____ Yes _____ No

   Are your sins forgiven? _____ Yes _____ No

How do you know that you have everlasting (eternal) life?

_____

_____

_____

9. For additional study, read each of the following verses and comment on what each of them means to you:

    ○ Ephesians 2:8–9

    ○ Romans 8:35–39

    ○ Titus 3:5

    ○ Philippians 1:6

10. *Our Daily Bread* is one of many devotional study guides. Daily Bible study helps you to grow in your relationship with Jesus Christ. For your spiritual encouragement, be faithful in reading the Bible references and thoughts in *Our Daily Bread.*[3] Or ask your helper to   recommend another devotional guide. Read your Bible daily.

11. First John 5:11–13 reminds the believer that God guarantees eternal life. It is a Bible passage on assurance of salvation. Commit 1 John 5:11–13 to memory. Then repeat the passage out loud to a Christian friend.

---

3 *Our Daily Bread* is a publication of RBC Ministries (Grand Rapids, Michigan).

Follow-Up (2) Your Life in Christ

My name is _____.

My helper's name and phone number is _____

_____.

Please read the following paragraph out loud:

The person who receives Jesus Christ as Savior is spiritually reborn (John 3:3, 7). Believers begin spiritual life as "newborn babes" (1 Peter 2:2). It is natural for babies to grow and develop. Believers must "grow in grace and in the knowledge of our Lord and Savior Jesus Christ" (2 Peter 3:18). Spiritual growth requires spiritual nourishment. The believer's primary source of nourishment is the Bible.

The purpose of this study is to discover from scripture how believers can grow through regular nourishment from God's Word. Read the scripture references given. Then place appropriate answers in the spaces provided.

1. How can believers grow in Jesus Christ?

   Spiritual "newborn babies" need the sincere _____
   of God's Word that growth might result (1 Peter 2:2).

   When spiritual babies become more mature, they can
   discern more difficult passages of scripture. These
   scripture passages are called the strong _____
   of God's Word (Hebrews 5:14)

   God's Word is _____ (John 17:17).

   God's Word is alive and powerful and is a _____
   of the thoughts and intents of the human heart (Hebrews
   4:12).

   God gave the Bible. It is profitable for _____,
   for _____, for _____, and
   for _____, in righteousness (2 Timothy 3:16).

   Believers must be diligent to be workmen who are not
   _____, rightly interpreting the word
   of truth (2 Timothy 2:15).

   The word of God's grace is able to make the believer
   strong (_____ _____ _____) and give
   you an _____ among all who are
   sanctified (Acts 20:32).

2. How can believers communicate with God?

God communicates His mind to believers through scripture. Believers communicate back to God through prayer. Prayer is talking to God. Prayer is the genuine believer's natural response to God (Romans 8:1; 1 John 4–5).

Paul said to _____ _____ _____ (1 Thessalonians 5:17). Through prayer, believers have immediate access to God. Believers can pray anytime.

Jesus said to _____, _____, and _____ and it shall be opened to us (Matthew 7:7). God responds to believers who pray.

Believers must make prayer requests in _____ believing that God will answer prayer (Matthew 21:22).

Believers must ask in the _____ of Jesus Christ (John 14:13). The name of Jesus is the summary statement of all that Jesus is. By closing your prayer, "In Jesus's name, amen," God's Son becomes involved in your prayer. (He identifies with your prayer.)

3. For what should believers pray?

Believers should pray for daily _____ (Matthew 6:11), for protection from being led into _____, and for deliverance from _____ (Matthew 6:13).

Believers should pray for _____ in dealing with the trials of life (James 1:5).

Paul prayed for other believers (Romans 1:9). He asked other believers to _____ for him (Romans 15:30–32).

Believers should pray that others would _____ on Jesus Christ in response to His Word being spoken (John 17:20).

Believers should pray for all who are in _____ (1 Timothy 2:2).

4. Begin a personal prayer diary. Include columns to record requests, the date the requests were made, how God answered those requests, and the date God answered each request.

5. David wrote, "Delight thyself also in the Lord: and He shall give thee the desires of thine heart" (Psalm 34:4). Believers must want what God wants. The will of God is a key essential to answered prayer. For additional study, draw lines connecting the following scripture passages to the appropriate references:

The Bible is a weapon known as "the sword of the Spirit."	Psalm 119:105
The Bible is a "lamp" unto our feet and a "light" unto our path.	Ephesians 6:17
The Bible is a "looking glass."	Psalm 126:5–6
The Bible is eternal and will "never pass away."	James 1:23
The Bible is "precious seed."	Matthew 24:35
The Bible is "sweeter than honey."	Jeremiah 23:29
The Bible is like "fire" to your soul.	Psalm 19:10
The Bible is "milk" providing spiritual nourishment.	1 Peter 2:2

6. For your encouragement, read your Bible daily, pray daily, and memorize a sequential listing of the books of the New Testament. (the table of contents of your Bible.)

The twenty-seven books of the New Testament are listed as follows:

Matthew	Ephesians	Hebrews
Mark	Philippians	James
Luke	Colossians	1 Peter
John	1 Thessalonians	2 Peter
Acts	2 Thessalonians	1 John
Romans	1 Timothy	2 John
1 Corinthians	2 Timothy	3 John
2 Corinthians	Titus	Jude
Galatians	Philemon	Revelation

Follow-Up (3) Your Walk with Christ

My name is _____.

My helper's name and phone number is _____

_____.

Please read the following paragraph out loud:

Believers have spiritual privileges and moral responsibilities. Believers are the "child[ren] of God" and are "joint-heirs" with Jesus Christ (Romans 8:16–17). Christians can "love one another" (1 John 4:7). A goal for each believer is conformity to Jesus Christ (Romans 12:1–2).

The purpose of this study is to describe your spiritual privileges and moral responsibilities. Read the scripture references given. Then place appropriate answers in the spaces provided.

1. Believers have the privilege of telling others about Jesus Christ.

The practice of telling others about Jesus Christ is called witnessing (Acts 1:8). If Jesus Christ is worth having, He is worth sharing with others. The Bible has much to say concerning the witness of believers.

Believers must be ready to give an _____ to every man who asks a reason of the _____ that is in you (1 Peter 3:15).

Proverbs 11:30 teaches that "he who wins _____ is wise."

The believer who goes forth with God-given sincerity, bearing the precious seed of the gospel, will doubtless come again with _____, bringing his _____ (new converts) with him (Psalm 126:6).

Acts 1:8 indicates that witnessing for Jesus Christ includes the following four geographical locations: _____ (your community), _____ (your county and state), _____ (your country), and the _____ _____ _____ _____ _____ (internationally to the continents beyond).

The believer has the responsibility to witness to _____ men "of what thou hast seen and heard" (Acts 22:15).

2. Believers have the privilege of waiting for the return of the Lord.

    God's true church is taken to heaven in the rapture (1 Thessalonians 4:13–17).[4] The promise of the rapture gives comfort to true believers (1 Thessalonians 4:18). Then we who are "alive and remain shall be _____ _____ (raptured) together with them in the clouds to meet the _____ in the air; and so shall we ever be with the _____" (1 Thessalonians 4:17).

    Jesus Christ has prepared a home in heaven for those who know Him as Savior. His promise is "I will _____ again" (John 14:3).

    Believers look for "that blessed hope," which is the glorious _____ of our Lord and Savior Jesus Christ (Titus 2:13).

3. Believers have the privilege of pleasing Jesus Christ. his involves guarding against temptation.

    When believers are tempted to do wrong, God provides a way of escape. "There hath no _____ taken you but such as is _____ to man; but God is _____, Who will not suffer you to be

---

4 The English word *rapture* does not appear in the KJV English translation. It is from a Latin term that means "to catch up" or "to be caught up."

_____ above that ye are able, but will with the temptation also make a _____ of escape that ye might be able to bear it" (1 Corinthians 10:13).

Temptation is a desire to think or do something that does not please God.

4. Read 1 Timothy 6:6–12. Comment on the passage in the space provided.

_____

_____

_____

_____

_____

_____

5. The Bible provides help in determining whether certain activities, attitudes, and thoughts are right or wrong. Use lines to match the following scripture references with the appropriate statements:

Will it glorify God?   1 Corinthians 10:31

Can it be done for the Lord?   Colossians 3:17

Can it be done in the name   Colossians 3:23
of the Lord?

Is it of that evil world system that opposes all that God represents?	1 Thessalonians 5:22
Are you in doubt about it?	1 John 2:15
Is it good in its appearance?	Romans 14:23
Would it hinder a fellow believer?	2 Corinthians 6:14
Will it form an unequal yoke with an unbeliever?	Romans 14:21
Could it become my master?	1 Corinthians 6:12
Is it God's will for my life?	James 4:15
Am I willing to face it in the Judgment? (Would I want to be involved in this activity when Jesus Christ comes again?)	2 Corinthians 5:10
Do I want to reap the fruit of this activity in my future life or in the lives of those I love?	Galatians 6:7

6. Practice witnessing by sharing Jesus Christ with others. The following is a sample plan of salvation that you can share with a friend.

Romans 3:10; 3:23   All have sinned.

Romans 5:12; 6:23   The consequence of sin is spiritual death which is separation from God forever.

Romans 5:6, 8   Jesus Christ endured the consequence of sin for sinners.

Romans 10:9, 10, 13; Sinners must receive Jesus Christ
John 1:12   as personal Lord and Savior.

7. From the following passages of scripture, in what other activities do believers participate? (This is an non exhaustive list.)

1 Corinthians 16:1–2 Believers g____ offerings to God.

Psalm 100:1–2   Believers s_____ the Lord with gladness and p_____ Hisname.

2 Timothy 2:15   Believers st_____ God's Word.

8. Memorize Psalm 119:11. "Thy Word have I hid in my heart that I might not sin against Thee."

Live in the power of the resurrected Lord.

Follow-Up (4) Your Fellowship with Christ and His People

My name is _____.

My helper's name and phone number is _____

_____.

Please read the following paragraph out loud:

Believers enjoy fellowship with God the Father, Jesus Christ, and with people who know the Lord (1 John 1:3). Fellowship is the sharing of a common bond with other believers and must be consistent with scripture (Romans 16:17–18; 2 Corinthians 6:14–7:1). Every believer needs fellowship.

The purpose of this study is to examine how believers can enjoy the fellowship God provides. Read the scripture references given. Then place appropriate answers in the spaces provided.

1. Is church attendance important?

   Believers are not to _____ the assembling
   of ourselves _____ as the manner of some
   is but to encourage one another through faithful church
   attendance because of the Lord's return (Hebrews 10:25).

   No one _____ to himself, and no one _____
   to himself (Romans 14:7). Believers are responsible for
   being faithful to God and others.

2. Believers have a responsibility to be baptized by immersion,
   following salvation.

   Is baptism a step of obedience to the command of Jesus
   Christ (Matthew 28:18–20)?
   _____ Yes _____ No

   The Bible records the instructions of Peter to a group of
   new Christians. "And he _____ them to be
   _____ in the name of the Lord Jesus" (Acts 10:48).

   How important is obedience to the commands of Jesus
   Christ (John 15:14)?

   _____

   How much water is necessary for baptism? John the
   Baptist went to Aenon because there was
   _____ water there (John 3:23).

Is water baptism necessary for salvation? (Ephesians 2:8–9.)
_____ Yes _____ No

A helpful class on believer's baptism is offered at the church. Why not arrange with the pastor or other church leadership to attend this class?

3. Believers have a responsibility to observe the Table of the Lord (communion).

    Who instituted the Table of the Lord (Matthew 26:26–28)?
    _____ _____

    The bread used in the communion service is *symbolic* of the _____ of Jesus Christ which was given for believers at Calvary (1 Corinthians 11:24). The cup, filled with grape juice, is *symbolic* of the _____ Jesus Christ shed on the cross for forgiveness of sins (1 Corinthians 11:25). Communion is observed in _____ of what Jesus Christ did at Calvary (1 Corinthians 11:24–25).

4. Believers have the responsibility to join a local church (church membership).

    Acts 2:41–42 lists a sequence of three important events in the lives of new believers. First, they gladly _____ the Word (salvation), then they were _____ (by immersion following salvation), and finally, they were _____ (joined as members) to the local church. These early believers formed a local fellowship. They became members of a local church. (Acts 1:15.)

In review, in what three events did the new believers participate?

    a. <u>Salvation</u>
    b. <u>B</u>
    c. <u>Church membership</u>

Following the successful completion of baptism class, the church offers a class on local church membership. You are invited to participate in this class.

5. For your encouragement, review the truths presented in the following lessons:

    ○ Your Faith in Jesus Christ
    ○ Your Life in Jesus Christ
    ○ Your Walk with Jesus Christ
    ○ Your Fellowship with Christ and His People

Review

6. For your growth, continue to read your Bible, pray daily, and memorize scripture passages relating to your walk with Christ. Also memorize, in sequential order, the names of the thirty-nine books of the Old Testament. A sequential listing of the Old Testament books is found in the table of contents of your Bible and as follows:

Genesis	Ecclesiastes
Exodus	Song of Solomon
Leviticus	Isaiah
Numbers	Jeremiah
Deuteronomy	Lamentations
Joshua	Ezekie
Judges	Daniel
Ruth	Hosea
1 Samuel	Joel
2 Samuel	Amos
1 Kings	Obadiah
2 Kings	Jonah
1 Chronicles	Micah
2 Chronicles	Nahum
Ezra	Habakkuk
Nehemiah	Zephaniah
Esther	Haggai
Job	Zechariah
Psalms	Malachi
Proverbs	

Answers to the Follow-Up Sessions (For the Discipler)

Session 1: Your Faith in Christ

Isaiah 53:6	Astray
John 3:18	Condemned
Romans 3:23	Come Short
Revelation 20:15	Lake of Fire
John 3:3, 7	Born Again
John 3:18	Not Condemned
2 Corinthians 5:17	Creation
1 Peter 2:2	Babe
1 John 2:12	Forgiven
1 John 5:13	Eternal Life
John 10:28	Perish
Romans 8:16	Spirit Sons/Children
1 Peter 1:5	God

All other answers should be reviewed by the discipler with his individual disciple.

Session 2: Your Life in Christ

1 Peter 2:2	Milk
Hebrews 5:14	Strong Meat
John 17:17	Truth
Hebrews 4:12	Discerner
2 Timothy 3:16	Doctrine, Reproof, Correction, Instruction
2 Timothy 2:15	Ashamed
Acts 20:32	(Build You Up), Inheritance
1 Thessalonians 5:17	Pray without Ceasing
Matthew 7:7	Ask, Seek, Knock
Matthew 21:22	Prayer/Faith
John 14:13	Name
Matthew 6:11–13	Bread/Daily Needs, Temptation, Evil
James 1:5	Wisdom
Romans 15:30–32	Pray
John 17:20	Believe
1 Timothy 2:2	Authority

Matching

The Bible is a weapon.	Ephesians 6:17
The Bible is a lamp.	Psalm 119:105
The Bible is a looking glass.	James 1:23
The Bible is eternal.	Matthew 24:35
The Bible is precious seed.	Psalm 126:5–6

The Bible is sweeter than honey. Psalm 19:10

The Bible is fire.   Jeremiah 23:29

The Bible is milk.   1 Peter 2:2

Session 3: Your Walk with Christ

1 Peter 3:15   Answer, Hope

Proverbs 11:30   Souls

Psalm 126:6   Rejoicing, Sheaves

Acts 1:8   Jerusalem, Judea, Samaria,
                          Uttermost Parts of the World

Acts 22:15   All

1 Thessalonians 4:17   Caught Up, Lord, Lord

John 14:3   Come

Titus 2:13   Appearing

1 Corinthians 10:13   Temptation, Common, Faithful,
                          Tempted, Way

1 Timothy 6:6–12   (Review the answers individually
                          from the text.)

Matching

Will it glorify God?   1 Corinthians 10:31

Can it be done for the Lord?   Colossians 3:23

Can it be in the Lord's name?   Colossians 3:17

Is it of the evil world system?   1 John 2:15

Are you in doubt about it?   Romans 14:23

Is it good in its appearance?	1 Thessalonians 5:22
Would it hinder a believer?	Romans 14:21
Will it form an unequal yoke?	2 Corinthians 6:14
Could it become my master?	1 Corinthians 6:12
Is it God's will?	James 4:15
Am I willing to be judged for it?	2 Corinthians 5:10
Do I want to reap its fruit?	Galatians 6:7
1 Corinthians 16:1–2	Give
Psalm 100:1–2	Serve, Praise
2 Timothy 2:15	Study

Session 4: Your Fellowship with Christ and His People

Hebrews 10:25	Forsake, Together
Romans 14:7	Lives, Dies
Matthew 28:18–20	Yes
Acts 10:48	Commanded, Baptized
John 15:14	Obedience demonstrates we are disciples of Jesus Christ.
John 3:23	Much
Ephesians 2:8–9	No
Matthew 26:26–28	Jesus Christ
1 Corinthians 11:24–25	Body, Blood, Remembrance
Acts 2:41–42	Received, Baptized, Added Salvation, Baptism, Membership

Spiritual Lessons for New Believers (Transitional Studies)

Baptism Class
Membership Class

Baptism Class (Leader's Guide)

A preacher just arrived at his first church. On his first Sunday, the church observed both ordinances (the Lord's Table and baptism). Because of the preacher's inexperience, he became nervous. He confused the ordinances. In the communion service, he said, "This do in the name of the Father, the Son, and Holy Spirit." In the baptismal service, to the wonderment of the candidate standing in the baptismal tank, he said, "Drink ye all of it."

Over the years, the doctrine of baptism has suffered greatly at the hands of confusion. Baptism class helps to clear up some of that confusion as you prepare to follow the Lord obediently in baptism.

Baptism class takes four plunges into the water of the Word. It addresses four topics on baptism.

1. The Must of Baptism

Commanded by Jesus Christ (Matthew 28:18–20)
Jesus Christ said, "Go ye therefore and [make disciples] of all nations, baptizing them in the name of

the Father, and of the Son, and of the Holy Spirit … and observe to do all that I command you (including obedience in baptism" (Matthew 28:19–20). To be obedient to the commandments of Jesus Christ, believers must obey His command for baptism.

Commanded for the Christian (Acts 8:38; 10:47–48)

Peter said unto them, "Repent, and [then] be baptized every one of you in the name of Christ Jesus [on the basis of] the remission (forgiveness) of sins" (Acts 2:38). When Cornelius was saved, Luke added, "Can any man forbid water that these should not be baptized that have received the Holy Spirit as well as we and he commanded them to be baptized in the name of the Lord" (Acts 10:47–48). Baptism is not an elective in the curriculum of the Christian life. It is not an option. It is an act of obedience for everyone who has repented in the name of Jesus Christ on the basis of forgiveness of sins. On the desert near modern-day Tel Aviv, an Ethiopian officer who had received Jesus Christ as Savior said, "What [does] hinder me from being baptized?" (Acts 8:36). Philip found no hindrances so "they both went down into the water" (Acts 8:38).

Believers have no valid reason for refusing baptism. Yet many believers give excuses. Some of the excuses are a lack of understanding as to what baptism is, indifference to the commandments of Jesus Christ, rebellion against Jesus Christ, a fear of water (Jesus Christ goes into the water with you and will not drown—and neither will you), old age (the pastor holds you up), waiting for a friend or a family member, a former church's teachings ("I was sprinkled as a baby"), tradition, and personal opinion (God's authority is greater than your authority: God's commandment is greater than your objections). What hinders you from being baptized?

Baptism was practiced in the early church. (Acts 2:41; 8:12, 36–38; 9:18; 10:47; 16:14–15, 33; 18:8; 19:5; 1 Corinthians 1:13–17.) It precedes church membership (Acts 2:41). Obedient believers obey the commandments of Jesus Christ (Matthew 28:18–20). The idea of an un-baptized believer was not entertained in the early church. Once saved, believers submitted to water baptism.

2. The Mode of Baptism

People sprinkle, dip, dunk, pour, immerse, and bob three times. A preacher and a woman stood together in the water of baptism in a church that believed in triune immersion (bobbing three times). Before taking the woman under the first time, the preacher asked, "Do you believe?" Before the woman could answer, he put her under the water, and as she came up, he asked a second time, "Do you believe?" Before she could answer, he put her under again. She came up and the preacher asked the third time, "Do you believe?" Again, before she could answer, the preacher put her under the water. The preacher asked the last time, "Do you believe?" After she came up, the woman responded, "Preacher, I believe you're trying to drown me."

What is the proper method (mode) of baptism? The proper method is determined in two ways:

by the meaning of the word *baptize* and by the method of baptism used in the Bible.

The Meaning of the Word *Baptize*

The English word *baptize* comes from a Greek word that is transliterated instead of translated. The Greek word *bapteezo* is found in Greek dictionaries. Liddell and Scott, two Anglicans, said bapteezo means to "to dip in or under water."[5] Thayer, a Congregationalist, said bapteezo means "to dip, to cleanse by dipping, to overwhelm, to immerse in water."[6] Bauer, Arnt, and Gingrech, German Reformed theologians, stated that bapteezo means "to dip, to immerse, to dip oneself, wash, plunge, sink, drench, overwhelm."[7]

In non-biblical early-Greek literature, the term *bapteezo* was used of dyeing and coloring clothes (by submerging material in a dye), drowning in a lake, and sinking a ship in the sea. In ancient literature, a war galley was "baptized" off Naples. It was not splashed or sprinkled. It was sunk. It never came up. In baptism, you will come up. You will survive.

In scripture, Luke used the term *bapteezo* to make reference to the baptisms of the Holy Spirit and fire (Luke 3:16). Paul used it of being placed into the church of Jesus Christ by the Holy Spirit (1 Corinthians 12:13). It was common to use the term to make reference to the earth being overwhelmed by

---

5 Henry George Liddell and Robert Scott, *A Greek-English Lexicon* (London: Oxford University Press, 1996), 305.

6 Joseph Henry Thayer, *Thayer's Greek-English Lexicon of the New Testament* (Grand Rapids: Zondervan, 1962), 95.

7 William Arnt and F. Wilbur Gingrech, *A Greek-English Lexicon of the New Testament* (London: The University of Chicago Press, 1957), 132.

God's fire of judgment (a traditional usage). It was used of Jesus when He was accused of not washing before dinner by not sinking His hands into a bowl of water (Luke 11:38), of the rich man in hell who asked Abraham to send Lazarus to dip the tip of his finger in water to cool his tormented tongue (Luke 16:24), of John the Baptist who was baptizing people in the Jordan River as he identified them with the coming of Jesus Christ (Matthew 3:5–6), and of Jesus Christ who was baptized in the Jordan (Mark 1:9).

Church leaders have commented on the meaning of the term *bapteezo*. John Calvin, the Presbyterian, said, "The word *bapteezo* signifies immersion. It is certain that immersion was the practice of the early church." Bishop Lightfoot, the Anglican, in commenting on a Bible baptism, said, "A person sinks beneath the baptismal water." Martin Luther, the Lutheran Reformer, said, "*Bapteezo* is a Greek word translated immerse. I would have all who would be baptized to be immersed." John Wesley, the Methodist, said, "Buried with Him in baptism. This alludes to the ancient manner of baptism by immersion." (This quote is taken from comments he made concerning Romans 6:3).[8]

What is the proper method of baptism? The meaning of the word indicates immersion. What about the method in the early church?

---

8 A collection of common quotations.

The Method of Baptism Used in the Bible

1. The Baptism of Jesus Christ

There are four references to the baptism of Jesus Christ in the gospels. They are Matthew 3:13–17; Mark 1:9–11; Luke 3:21–22; and John 1:31–34. In each, Jesus Christ goes down into the Jordan River and comes out to see the heavens open and the Holy Spirit like a dove descending upon Him. For example, in Mark 1:9–11, the gospel writer noted,

It came to pass in those days, that Jesus came from Nazareth of Galilee and was baptized of John in the Jordan. And straightway coming up out of the water He saw the heavens opened and the Spirit like a dove descending upon Him and there came a voice from heaven saying, "Thou art My beloved Son in Whom I am well pleased."

2. The Baptism of John the Baptist (John the Baptizer)

The purpose of John's baptism was for people to identify with the coming Messiah. "And John also was baptizing in Aenon near to Salim, because there was much water there: and they came and were baptized" (John 3:23). If sprinkling was the method of baptism, they could have stopped at a well. But because baptism is by immersion and requires much water, they baptized in the Jordan River. At that site, the depth of the river is five to twelve feet deep.

3. Christian Baptism

In Acts 2:41, 3,000 souls were baptized. How? Jerusalem has hundreds of pools including Siloam and Bethesda. There is enough water. Twelve disciples would require six to eight hours to baptize 3,000 people. Baptism requires water. So does immersion.

In Acts 8:36–38, the Ethiopian officer stopped his chariot beside much water, He said, due to his salvation, "What doth hinder me from being baptized? . . . And he commanded the chariot to stand still, and they both went down into the water, both Philip and the Ethiopian officer, and he baptized him … then they came up out of the water." Baptism requires much water. So does immersion.

In Acts 10:47–48, the question of Cornelius was "Can any forbid water that these should not be baptized?" An adult asked the question. Adult believers are immersed by water as well as children who believe.

In Acts 16:13–15, Lydia and her household received Jesus Christ by a riverside and were baptized. There was much water there.

In Romans 6:3–5, the order of baptism is pictured as death: standing before observers in identification with what happened at Calvary; burial: going under the water; and resurrection: coming up out of the water. Immersion is the only baptismal method which pictures completely identification with the death, burial, and resurrection of Jesus Christ.

No passage of scripture mentions sprinkling, pouring, or baby christening, yet there is an abundance of evidence for baptism by immersion.[9] Baptism requires water (Matthew 3:11). Immersion requires water (Matthew 3:11). Baptism requires much water (John 3:23). Immersion requires much water (John 3:23). Baptism requires a "going into" (Acts 8:38). Immersion requires a "going into" (Acts 8:38). Baptism requires a "coming out of" (Acts 8:39). Immersion requires a "coming out of" (Acts 8:39). Baptism is a form of burial (Romans 6:4). Immersion is a form of burial (Romans 6:4). Baptism is a form of resurrection (Colossians 2:12). Immersion is a form of resurrection (Colossians 2:12).

The second-century AD chapel on Mount Nebo in Jordan has a baptistry pool. It is large enough to perform a baptism by immersion. The variety of evidence is overwhelming that the mode of baptism in the early church was immersion.

3. The Message of Baptism

What are the purposes of Christian baptism? There are three purposes.

1. Baptism pictures salvation.

Baptism does not save. Baptism is not a sacrament. It is not a substitute for the Old Testament practice of circumcision. Baptism has nothing to do with entering a covenantal

---

9 In my travels, at the various holy sites in Israel and Jordan, baptismal wells remain where early generation converts were immersed (at Mt. Nebo, Gadara, and other sites). Even the Jews had their Mikveh (bath site for Judaism's ritual cleansing). Tour guides admit to immersion as the New Testament's method of baptism.

relationship with God. Baptism does not save. It is merely a way for believers to say publicly, "I am saved." Baptism is not salvation. It is a picture of salvation by which believers identify publicly with what happened through the death, burial, and resurrection of Jesus Christ.

In the New Testament, baptism follows salvation. This sequence is seen in several passages. Peter said, "Repent and [then] be baptized every one of you [on the basis of] the remission of sins" (Acts 2:38). Luke wrote, "Then they that gladly received His Word were baptized" (Acts 2:41). Luke added, "But when they believed … they were baptized" (Acts 8:12). The Ethiopian said, "What doth hinder me from being baptized?" Philip said, "If thou believest with all thine heart, thou mayest." And he answered and said, "I believe that Jesus Christ is the Son of God." And he commanded the chariot to stand still: and they both went down into the water (he was baptized). (Acts 8:36–38). Of Cornelius and his family, Luke wrote, "Those who had received the Holy Spirit were commanded [to be] baptized in the name of the Lord" (Acts 10:47–48). When the Philippian jailer believed, he was "baptized, he and all his, straightway" (Acts 16:33–34). When Crispus and many of the Corinthians believed, they "were baptized" (Acts 18:8). When people believed on Jesus Christ, they were "baptized in the name of the Lord Jesus" (Acts 19:4–5).

The sequence is always salvation first and baptism second. Baptism follows salvation. Scripture says that salvation requires belief and confession. The christening of babies does not fulfill the sequential requirements given in God's Word (public identification with the death, burial, and resurrection of Jesus).[10]

2. Baptism is a symbol (picture of salvation).

Presenter: Hold up a picture of a red wagon or some other object. Ask, "What is this?" When the respondents say, "A red wagon," you say, "Can you ride in it?" The respondents will say, "No." You say, "Why not?" The respondents will say," Because it is not real. It is only a picture." You say, "That is correct. It is only a picture. It is not the real thing. So too with baptism. It is only a picture of our salvation in Jesus Christ. Baptism does not save."

Or you can hold up a picture of a lion and adapt your questions to the picture of the lion. This time you can hold your hand next to the lion's mouth and say, "Ouch! It bit me!" Those attending baptism class will say, "The lion did not bite you." Ask, "Why?" They will respond, "Because it is not a lion. It is a picture of a lion." Then explain that baptism is a picture of salvation and does not provide salvation for sinners.

Another idea is to stroke the wool on a picture of a lamb. "Did I stroke the lamb's wool?" "No." Why not?" It is only a picture.

10 Christening began when Rome declared Christianity the state religion. The emperor's advisors equated circumcision with salvation. Circumcision was considered too gruesome. Since large numbers of people were being initiated at once, sprinkling replaced circumcision. When christened, people thought they were placed under a covenant of grace. They were not. The practice ushered in the Dark Ages, which lasted 1,000 years.

Through a believer's baptism, the believer identifies with Jesus Christ in three ways.

1. The believer identifies with the death of Jesus Christ (Romans 6:3).

Paul wrote, "Know ye not that so many of us as were baptized into Jesus Christ were baptized into His death?" (Romans 6:3). When the candidate for baptism stands before the congregation, he confesses that he identifies with what Jesus Christ did on the cross. Jesus Christ died for sins.

2. The believer identifies with the burial of Jesus Christ (Romans 6:4).

Paul wrote, "Therefore, we are buried with Him by baptism into death" (Romans 6:4). The only form of baptism that pictures the burial of Jesus Christ is immersion. Burial requires being placed under the elements. Through immersion, a burial is pictured. Paul wrote, "Buried with Him in baptism, wherein ye are also raised with Him through the faith of the operation of God Who hath raised Him from the dead" (Colossians 2:12).

3. The believer identifies with the resurrection of Jesus Christ (Romans 6:5).

Paul wrote, "For if (since) we have been planted together in the likeness of His death, we shall also in the likeness of His resurrection" (Romans 6:5). When the candidate for baptism is taken out of the water, it pictures the resurrection of Jesus Christ. The believer identifies publicly with the new life he has in Jesus Christ.

Baptism is a public testimony by the believer that he has received Jesus Christ as Savior. Participation in baptism is a witness in itself. It preaches a silent message, in a public way, that baptized believer is saved.

3. Baptism precedes church membership.

The sequence in Acts 2:41 is belief, baptism, and church membership. The original language indicates that those who were baptized "joined" the local church on that same day. That first local church had 120 charter members. (Acts 1:15.)

Early baptism was an initiation into church membership. Believers who separate baptism from church membership lose some of the significance of the act.

4. The Manner of Baptism

Baptism is by immersion following salvation. The sequence at the church is salvation, baptism class, membership class, a meeting with the church leadership (to share the testimony of conversion), a vote of approval by the membership of the church (contingent on baptism), the baptism, and church membership.

Baptism Class (Study Guide)

Introduction: Baptism by immersion following salvation is one of the first acts of obedience for every believer. To help explain this elementary doctrine, this first-steps study takes four plunges into the water of the Word.

1. The Must of Baptism

   o Baptism is commanded by Jesus Christ (Matthew 28:18–20).

   o Baptism is commanded for the Christian (Acts 10:47–48).

2. The Mode of Baptism

   o The Meaning of the Word *Baptize*

   o The Method of Baptism in the Bible

1. The Baptism of Jesus (Mark 1:9–11)

2. Baptism by John (John 3:23)

3. The Baptism of Believers (Acts 8:36–38)

3. The Message of Baptism

    A. Baptism pictures salvation.

        1. Baptism does not save (Acts 8:12, 36–38; 18:8).

        2. Baptism is a symbol (Romans 6:3–5).

    B. Baptism precedes church membership (Acts 2:41).

4. The Manner of Baptism at This Church

Notes

Baptism Class Study Helps

New Testament Passages on Baptism (all types)

- Matthew 3:6, 7, 11, 16; 21:25; 28:19
- Mark 1:4, 5, 8, 9; 10:38, 39; 11:30; 16:16
- Luke 3:3, 7, 12, 16, 21; 7:29; 12:50; 20:4
- John 1:25–33; 3:22, 23, 26; 4:1; 10:40
- Acts 1:5, 22; 2:38, 41; 8:12, 16, 36–39
- Acts 10:37, 47, 48; 11:16; 13:24; 16:14, 15, 33, 34. 18:8
- Acts 18:25; 19:3, 5; 22:16
- Romans 6:3–5
- 1 Corinthians 1:13–17; 10:2; 12:13; 15:29
- Galatians 3:27
- Ephesians 4:5
- Colossians 2:12
- 1 Peter 3:21

The Meaning of the Word *Baptism* in Greek Lexicons (Dictionaries)

- Liddel and Scott: "to dip in or under water"
- Thayer: "to dip, to cleanse by dipping, to immerse in water, to overwhelm"
- Bauer, Arnt, and Gingrech: "to dip, immerse, dip oneself, wash, plunge, sink, drench, overwhelm"

Comments by Church Leaders

- John Calvin: "The word 'baptism' signifies immersion. It is certain that immersion was the practice of the early church."
- Bishop Lightfoot: "The (person) sinks beneath the baptismal water."
- Martin Luther: "Baptizo is a Greek word translated 'immerse'. I would have those who are to be baptized to be altogether immersed."
- John Wesley: "Buried with Him in baptism. This alludes to the ancient manner of baptism by immersion."

Baptism Requires	Scripture Cited	Immersion Requires
Water	Matthew 3:11	Water
Much water	John 3:23	Much water
Going into	Acts 8:38	Going into
Coming out of	Acts 8:39	Coming out of
Form of burial	Romans 6:3–4	Form of burial
Form of resurrection	Colossians 2:12	Resurrection

Questions Concerning Baptism

1. Explain why baptism does not save. Of what is baptism symbolic? (What does it picture?) What mode or form best suits this picture?

2. Have you been baptized? Do you desire to be baptized?

3. Explain the relationship between baptism and church membership (Acts 2:41).

4. In the space remaining on this page, record your personal testimony of salvation. (Use scripture references where appropriate.)

Membership Class (Leader's Guide)

Luke wrote,

> Then they that gladly received his word were baptized and the same day there were added (joined) unto them about 3,000 souls. They continued steadfastly in the apostles' doctrine (teachings) and fellowship and in the breaking of bread and in prayers, and fear came upon every soul and many wonders and signs were done by Christ's apostles. All that believed were together and they had all things common. They sold their possessions and goods and parted them to all men as every man had need. They continued daily with one accord in the temple and, breaking bread from house to house, did eat their meat with gladness and singleness of heart, praising God and having favor with all the people, and the Lord added to the church daily such as should be saved (Acts 2:41–47).

The church, in first-century times, was built on the right foundation (Acts 2:42), met for fellowship

(Acts 2:42), had faith in God (Acts 2:42), feared God (Acts 2:43), distributed finances among the needy (Acts 2:44–45), had a fervor for God (Acts 2:46–47), had favor among the people in their community (Acts 2:47), and bore biblical spiritual fruit (Acts 2:47).

Membership is defined as the commitment of a believer to the fellowship of the local church. In salvation, the believer identifies with the person of Jesus Christ. Through membership, the believer identifies with the people of Jesus Christ.

Membership class has two parts. Part 1 focuses attention on the Christian who desires to join the church. Part 2 focuses attention on the church the Christian desires to join.

Part 1: The Christian Who Desires to Join the Church

Privileges of the Christian

The Christian enjoys two tremendous privileges.

The first is the privilege of being a member of the universal church.

The universal church is the body of Jesus Christ comprised of all true believers throughout history, regardless of location or circumstance. Only true believers belong to the universal church. In addressing a group of believers, Paul wrote,

For as the body is one and has members. And all the members of that one body, being many, are

one body, so also is Christ. For by one spirit are we all (placed into) baptized into one body. Whether we be Jews or Gentiles, whether we be bond or free: and have been made to drink into one spirit. For the body is not one member, but many. (1 Corinthians 12:12–14)

Once saved, believers were added to the local church. Luke wrote, "And believers were the more added unto the Lord (the universal church), multitudes both of men and women."

The second is the privilege of becoming a member of a local church.

A local church is a called-out assembly of born-again believers having officers, meeting together to observe the ordinances, and worshipping Jesus Christ. New Testament local churches met at the following places: Jerusalem (Acts 8:1), Antioch (Acts 13:1), Cenchrea (Romans 16:1), Corinth (2 Corinthians 1:1), Philadelphia (Revelation 3:7), and in other locations (Galatia, Thessalonica, Sardis, Ephesus, and elsewhere). Early believers were members of local churches.

John wrote,

That which we have seen and heard declare we unto you, that ye also may have fellowship (partnership and participation) with us: and truly our fellowship (partnership and participation) is with the Father, and with His Son Jesus Christ. And these things write we unto you, that your joy may be full. (1 John 1:3–4)

The New Testament never questions local church membership. Church membership was not an option. Believers who were not members of local churches were aberrations. Every believer became a member of a local church. New Testament books were addressed to local churches. Professing Christ as Savior results in fellowship with other believers and a commitment to His church. (Acts 2:41–47.)

Luke wrote, "Then they that gladly received His word were baptized: and the same day there were added unto them about 3,000 souls. And the Lord added to the church daily such as should be saved" (Acts 2:41; 2:47). The sequence is belief, baptism, then church membership. One hundred twenty people were members of the first local church.

Local church membership is implied in the following New Testament passages:

Acts 1:15; 2:41; 4:4   The number of members was known, implying a membership roll.

Acts 6:2–5   The election of deacons, the first church officers, necessitates membership roll.

Acts 15:22   Business was transacted in the early church. This assumes a membership roll to determine a quorum and to conduct business.

1 Corinthians 5:13	Church discipline assumes a roll. A member was not excluded from membership in the universal church. This would involve the loss of salvation. Instead, a sinning member was excluded from attending the ordinary meetings of the church until that person repented of the sin. To be put out, one must have been taken in.
1 Timothy 5:9	Special requirements for membership were given. Widows under sixty years of age were not permitted to be taken into the membership of the local church. The reason is given in verse 11. "But the younger widows refuse, for when they have begun to *wax wanton* against Christ, they will marry." Christ wants a pure church with a godly testimony for Him.

Isolation leads to inefficiency. God established the local church for every believer. There are no exceptions. Believers need fellowship. Charcoal on a grill, separated from the fire, will turn gray and become cool. When it is joined to live coals, it becomes red and gives off heat. Coals work best with other coals. The best way to know God is together. Warmth of fellowship is found through membership in a local church.

Principles for the Christian

Requirements for Membership

The Bible reveals two requirements for membership (Acts 2:41).

The first is belief.

Joe goes to church. He was baptized as a baby. He is a member of a church. He walked the aisle at an evangelistic crusade. Joe lives in a Christian nation. He has Christian friends. He was raised in a Christian family. He lives in a Christian home. Joe is a moral person. He keeps the Ten Commandments, obeys the golden rule, and serves in his church. Joe prays, reads his Bible, gives money to the church, likes the pastor, and loves the Lord. Has anything been said about Joe that confirms he is saved? No.

Salvation is not what people get by keeping the Ten Commandments, by going to church, by loving Christ and others, or by being christened as a baby, nor do people acquire salvation by giving to the poor. Salvation is by grace through faith. It is through receiving Jesus Christ as personal Savior (John 1:12).

Of the point in time when a sinner becomes saved, Paul wrote,

> That if thou shalt confess with thy mouth the Lord Jesus, and shalt believe in thine heart that God hath raised Him from the dead, thou shalt

be saved. For with the heart man believeth unto righteousness: and with the mouth confession is made unto Salvation. For whosoever shall call upon the name of the Lord, shall be saved. (Romans 10:9–13)

"Confess" means to agree with God concerning our sin. "Believe" means to trust God to forgive us of our sin and give us eternal life. Salvation is more than believing the facts concerning Jesus Christ. It is having faith in Jesus Christ. Since there is a point in time *before* salvation and a point in time *after* salvation, there is a point in time *of* salvation. When grappling with issues of the assurance of salvation, it is helpful for the believer to know the point in time when he or she received Jesus Christ as Savior.

Blondin was a tightrope walker. He walked across a tightrope above Niagara Falls. A crowd gathered. Blondin asked the crowd if they thought he could wheel a wheelbarrow across the tightrope. The crowd responded enthusiastically. Blondin asked the crowd if they thought he could wheel the wheelbarrow across the tightrope with a person in the wheelbarrow. The crowd responded enthusiastically. Blondin asked for a volunteer. No one responded. The crowd believed the fact that Blondin could accomplish the feat. But no one was willing to trust his life to Blondin's wheelbarrow. James wrote, "The devils believe and tremble" (James 2:19). They believe the facts about Jesus. But they do not entrust their eternal destiny to Him. Only Christ can get your soul from earth to heaven. Trust your eternal destiny to Jesus by placing saving faith in Him.

The second is the believer's baptism.

Of the seven baptisms mentioned in scripture (three in the Old Testament, three in the New Testament, and one between the Testaments), believer's baptism is not baptism as a baby (never mentioned in scripture), Noah's symbolic baptism in the Flood (1 Peter 3:18–21), Moses's symbolic baptism in the cloud and in the Red Sea (1 Corinthians 10:1–4), the baptism of Christ in the River Jordan (Matthew 3:16–17), the baptism of fire (Matthew 3:11–12), Holy Spirit baptism by which God places us into the body of Christ (1 Corinthians 12:13), or the baptism of suffering by which James and John would identify with the commitments expected by Christ (Matthew 20:20–23). Believer's baptism is a public testimony of faith, by immersion in water, following salvation. Baptism does not save. It is a symbol, picture, and public testimony of a believer's salvation. It precedes membership in a New Testament local church (Acts 2:41).

Responsibilities of the Member

Members have many privileges. Some of those privileges are as follows:

- voting in business meetings
- teaching
- holding office
    - being part of a local church

With every privilege there are responsibilities. Some of those responsibilities are as follows:

Conduct.

Each member must conduct himself or herself in daily life so as to give evidence of being in agreement with the articles of faith (Galatians 5:13).

Consistency.

Each member should attend the services of the church (Hebrews 10:24–25).

Commitment.

Each member should volunteer his or her services within the limits of his or her abilities (Ephesians 6:7).

Concern.

Each member should pray for the leadership of the local church (1 Thessalonians 5:12–13).

Cultivation.

Each member should cultivate brotherly love for all members of the church (1 John 4:7–8).

Continuity.

Each member should live a life consistent with the character qualities of Jesus Christ (1 Corinthians 12:26–27).

Part 2: The Church the Christian Desires to Join

This session is divided into the following three parts: beliefs, bylaws, and becoming a member.

Beliefs

Articles of Faith (see the appropriate pages in your church's constitution.)

Baptist Distinctives (for those in a Baptist church)

When shopping for cereal at a grocery store, people look at labels. Few people would buy cereal without a label on the box. Churches have labels. If your church is Baptist, what do Baptists believe?

There are eight Baptist Distinctives.

1. B: Biblical Authority (2 Timothy 2:16–17)

The Bible is the sole basis for faith and practice. The Bible is the believer's sole authority because it is the Word of God.

2. A: Autonomy of the Local Church (1 Timothy 3:15)

God rules the church. He is the Lord of the church. Autonomous local churches are governed from within. Local church governments are congregational with each member having an equal vote.

3. P: Priesthood of all Believers (Revelation 1:5–6)

Every believer is a priest. A priest is someone who has direct access to God.

A small boy entered an executive's office. He walked past the secretary, waved at the people in the waiting room, and entered the executive's office. Why did the boy have direct access? The boy was the executive's son. Believers are related to God. As God's spiritual children, believers have direct access to God.

4. T: Two Ordinances (Acts 2:41–42)

An ordinance is a commandment to be obeyed. The two ordinances are believer's baptism (Acts 10:47–48) and the Lord's Table (1 Corinthians 11:23–30). Neither ordinance saves. Each must be administered in the context of the local church.

5. I: Individual Soul Liberty (Romans 14:5)

Each believer, indwelt by the Holy Spirit, can act as led by the Holy Spirit.

6. S: Saved Church Membership (Acts 2:41–47)

Local church membership is limited to believers only. Only believers are indwelt by the

Holy Spirit. At business meetings or conference sessions, the Holy Spirit votes through believers. Local churches, with saved church members, are led by the Holy Spirit.

7. T: Two Offices (Philippians 1:1; 1 Timothy 3)

The two offices are pastor and deacon. The pastor leads and feeds the flock of God (1 Peter 5:1–4). Deacons assist in the work of the ministry (Acts 6:1–7). The qualifications for these offices are given in 1 Timothy 3 and Titus 1.

8. S: Separation of Church and State (Matthew 22:21)

The governments of man and God are distinct (Romans 13:1–7). When God and government agree, believers must obey both God and the government. When God and government disagree, believers must obey God.

Church Covenant

The church covenant is found on the appropriate page or pages of your church constitution. It is an agreement by the membership.

The Bylaws of This Church

The bylaws are found on the appropriate pages of your church constitution.

The Church Constitution

The constitution is a document stating the principles, laws, and organizational structure of the local church. It is a set of guidelines to be practiced.

Commitment to Missionaries

Many churches are committed to home and international missions (Acts 1:8). Please refer to the missionary listing provided by your church.

Becoming a Member

The following are the steps required for membership at this church:

- baptism by immersion following salvation
- membership class
- meeting with the church leadership
- motion and approval by the church
- membership

Membership Class (Study Guide)

Introduction: Membership is the commitment of a believer to the fellowship of a local church. Through salvation the believer identifies with the Person of Jesus Christ. Through membership the believer identifies with the people of Jesus Christ. This study presents two topics related to membership.

The Christian Who Desires to Join the Church

Privileges of the Christian

- the privilege of being a member of the universal church
  1 Corinthians 2:12–14; Acts 5:14

- The privilege of becoming a member of a local church
  1 John 1:3–4; Acts 2:41, 47

Principles for the Christian

- requirements for membership   Acts 2:41
- responsibilities of the member   Acts 1:14

The Church the Believer Joins

Beliefs (ABC's)

- Articles of Faith
- Baptist Distinctives (for those in a Baptist church)
- Covenant of the Church

Bylaws

- Constitution
- Commitment to Missionaries

Becoming a Member

- baptism by immersion following salvation
- membership class
- meeting with the church leadership
- motion and approval by the church
- membership

Notes

Spiritual Lessons for New Believers (Addendum)

How to Study the Bible
Answers to How to Study the Bible

How to Study the Bible

A disciple is one who follows Jesus Christ. A Christ follower who spent daily time with Jesus wrote, "But grow in grace and in the knowledge of our Lord and Savior Jesus Christ. To Him be glory both now and forever. Amen" (2 Peter 3:18). For the purpose of spiritual growth, all believers need to study the Bible. A thorough study of God's Word strengthens the believer's trust in God (grace) and acquaints believers with the truths of God (knowledge). Time spent in prayer, Bible study, meditation, and the application of God's Word is called a believer's devotional life (a quiet time with God). To have that quiet time with God, the believer should establish a place to pray and study (Mark 1:35), have a plan for prayer and study (Luke 14:28), and designate an available period of time for prayer and study (Psalm 119:147–148).

The purpose of this study is to answer five questions about a personal quiet time with God, with emphasis on the believer's time spent in God's Word. An additional study devoted specifically to prayer can be found in Keith D. Pisani's discipleship content book

Spiritual Lessons for Growing Believers published by WestBow Press.[11]

Why Should Believers Have a Quiet Time with God?

Daily Bible study benefits believers for the following reasons. (Look up the following passages of scripture. Describe the benefit a study of God's Word provides for the believer. Refer to the listings at the end of this session for this study's answers.)

Joshua 1:6–8   (_____) in God's Word is the key to success.

Joshua had one option for God's people Israel: win. Defeat meant annihilation. Joshua wrote,

> Be strong and of a good courage: for unto this people shalt thou divide for an inheritance the land, which I sware unto their fathers to give them. Only be thou strong and very courageous, that thou mayest observe to do according to all the law, which Moses my servant commanded thee: turn not from it to the right hand or to the left, that thou mayest prosper withersoever thou

---

11 The lesson "How to Study the Bible" is taken from "Q: Quiet Time" in Keith D. Pisani's book *Spiritual Lessons for Growing Believers*, which is published by WestBow Press and is available through the publisher and the author's website: www.keithpisaniministries.com.

goest. This book of the law shall not depart out of thy mouth; but thou shalt meditate therein day and night, that thou mayest observe to do according to all that is written therein: for then thou shalt make thy way prosperous, and then thou shalt have good success. (Joshua 1:6–8)

The wisdom derived from God's Word gives the believer an edge in analyzing situations and actions. It is the key to winning or losing in life.

Psalm 119:9, 11   It keeps a believer from (   ).

Wherewithal shall a young man cleanse his way? By taking heed thereto according to Thy Word. With my whole heart have I sought Thee: O let me not wander from Thy commandments. Thy Word have I hid in mine heart, that I might not sin against Thee.

(The term "hid" means to "treasure up" as a priceless possession.)

Either sin will keep the believer from the Bible or the Bible will keep the believer from sin. Study God's Word. It helps keep the believer separated (set apart) from bad thoughts and wrongdoing.

Psalm 119:105, 130   It shines a (   ) on hard-to-understand matters.

"Thy Word is a lamp unto my feet, and a light unto my path … The entrance of Thy words giveth light; it giveth understanding unto the simple" (Psalm 119:105, 130). An Old Testament oil "lamp" was worn on the toe of a person's sandal. It gave light for one step at a time. A light was a torch or other device that gave illumination for an extended length of time and distance. God's Word penetrates the darkness. It provides light for the believer's journey through life.

Proverbs 2:1–5 It provides a source of spiritual (_____).

> My son, if thou wilt receive my words, and hide my commandments with thee; So that thou incline thine ear unto wisdom, and apply thine heart to understanding; Yea, if thou criest after knowledge, and liftest up thy voice for understanding; If thou seekest her as silver, and searchest for her as for hid treasures; Then shalt thou understand the fear of the LORD, and find the knowledge of God. (Proverbs 2:1–5)

One possession every believer needs is spiritual discernment. The source of discernment is the wisdom of God. Wisdom comes from God (James 1:2–4) and His Word (Proverbs 1:1–7). To obtain the wisdom given by God, believers must study God's Word. Applied wisdom takes the guesswork out of life.

Jeremiah 15:16   <u>It brings God's (   ) to the believer's life.</u>

"Thy words were found, and I did eat them; and Thy Word was unto me the joy and rejoicing of mine heart: for I am called by Thy name, O Lᴏʀᴅ God of hosts" (Jeremiah 15:16). When Jeremiah found the scroll of God's Word, he took it into his system, digested its truths, and the spiritual nourishment he received changed his life. (When it hit his stomach, it made *the* difference in his life.) To receive nourishment from God's Word, the believer must drink the milk (1 Peter 2:2) and eat the meat (Hebrews 5:14) of God's Word. Live on the strength of the Word.

Acts 17:10–14   <u>It adds (   ) to life.</u>

> And the brethren immediately sent away Paul and Silas by night unto Berea: who coming thither went into the synagogue of the Jews. These were more noble than those in Thessalonica, in that they received the Word with all readiness of mind, and searched the scriptures daily, whether those things were so. Therefore many of them believed; also of honorable women which were Greeks, and of men, not a few. But when the Jews of Thessalonica had knowledge that the Word of God was preached of Paul at Berea, they came thither also, and stirred up the people. (Acts 17:10–14)

God's Word, publicly proclaimed, makes unbelievers nervous and angry. Upset people *upset people*. Even so, the Bereans remained steadfast in their love for the Word. Presenters who dilute the message of scripture and replace it with popular opinions and philosophy do the church a major disservice. Only God's Word brings eternal security to a person's life. Make time for God by making time for His Word.

1 Peter 2:2   <u>It results in spiritual (</u>   <u>)</u>.

"As newborn babes, desire the sincere milk of the word, that ye may grow thereby …" (1 Peter 2:2). Physical bodies that remain the size of babies (people who never grow) are an aberration. Believers are born to grow. Christians who remain spiritual infants are immature in their faith. How much spiritual growth have you experienced since you were saved? What stunts your spiritual growth? Have you continued to grow, or does your personal growth chart indicate that you have "shrunk" in your faith?

2 Timothy 2:15   <u>It allows believers to (</u>   <u>)</u>
                     <u>God's command to (</u>   <u>)</u>
                     <u>His Word</u>.

"Study to shew thyself approved unto God, a workman that needeth not to be ashamed, rightly dividing the Word of truth" (2 Timothy 2:15). To "rightly divide" means to "cut the furrow straight." There is one proper interpretation of God's Word (God's interpretation; 2 Peter 1:19–21).

When studying God's Word, compare scripture with scripture. This allows for a more consistent interpretation of Bible passages. In life, instead of asking, "What would Jesus do?" ask, "What does the Bible say?" What Jesus would do is open to speculation. What the Bible says is black ink on white paper. (It is clear.)

In a verse entitled "My Bible and I," a poet wrote,

> We've traveled together, my Bible and I,
> Through all kinds of weather, with smile or with sigh!
> In sorrow or sunshine, in tempest or calm!
> Thy friendship unchanging, my lamp and my psalm.
>
> Oh, no, my dear Bible, exponent of light!
> Thou sword of the Spirit, put error to flight!
> And still through life's journey, until my last sigh,
> We'll travel together, my Bible and I.[12]

A quiet time is a time of prayer, study, meditation, and application of God's Word. To have a quiet time, the believer must have a place (Mark 1:35), a plan (Luke 14:28), and an available period of time (Psalm 119:147–148). The purpose of this study is to answer four questions about a personal quiet time with God, with emphasis on the believer's time spent in God's Word. (For insights on prayer, see the chapter on Prayer in Keith D. Pisani's discipleship content book *Spiritual Lessons for Growing Believers* published by WestBow Press.)

---

12 Eleanor Doan, *Speaker's Sourcebook* (Grand Rapids, MI: Zondervan, 1960), 34–35.

What Should Believers Include When Having a Quiet Time with God?

Pick up your Bible. How securely can you grasp it with one finger? How securely can you grasp it with two fingers? You cannot grasp your Bible securely until you get a firm grip with your whole hand. How should believers grab hold of the Word? A hand illustration is an easy-to-remember training tool on getting a firm grasp on the scriptures. (Draw an outline of your hand on a blank piece of paper. Then label each finger with the five words listed in this study.)[13] The following are five methods believers can use to learn from the scriptures. (Use the five key terms listed below to complete the hand illustration; refer to the addendum at the end of this study for this session's answers.)

Romans 10:17   (H_____) the Word.

Paul wrote, "So then faith cometh by hearing, and hearing by the Word of God" (Romans 10:17). People retain 5 percent of what they hear. Hearing is the least effective method of retention. The weakest finger (the pinkie) represents hearing. Hearing the Word from trained teachers and godly pastors provides valuable insights into God's Word. Believers can hear the Word in church (preaching service, Sunday school, small groups, Bible studies), on electronic devices (over the air, over media connections), and through word of mouth.

---

13 The hand illustration is an adaptation of a popular training tool appearing often in the public sector.

Revelation 1:3   (R_____) the Word.

John wrote, "Blessed is he that readeth, and they that heareth the words of this prophecy, and keepeth those things that are written therein: for the time is at hand" (Revelation 1:3). Reading gives an overall picture of the Bible. Reading is an essential ingredient in experiencing a quality quiet time. People retain 15 percent of what they read. Reading is represented by the ring (fourth) finger. Believers are guaranteed a blessing from God when they read God's Word.

Acts 17:11   (S_____) the Word.

Luke reported that the believers at Berea "searched the scriptures daily, as to whether those things were so" (Acts 17:11). Studying requires a greater investment of time and results in an increase in Bible knowledge. Most people retain 35 percent of what they study. This method is represented by the middle finger.

Psalm 119:9, 11   (M_____) the Word.

The psalmist wrote, "Wherewithal shall a young man cleanse his way? By taking heed thereto according to Thy word … Thy word have I hid in my heart that I might not sin against Thee" (Psalm 119:9, 11). "Hid" means to "treasure up and count as precious." For the believer who memorizes God's Word, the Holy Spirit brings to remembrance appropriate verses to help the believer through times of trial or temptation. Scripture memory stimulates meaningful meditation. People who consistently review what they memorized remember 100 percent of the memorized passages. The index finger, which is the strongest finger, represents scripture memorization. How much of scripture have you memorized?

Psalm 1:1–2   (M_____) on God's Word.

David wrote,

> Blessed is the man who walketh not in the counsel of the ungodly, nor standeth in the way of sinners, nor sitteth in the seat of the scornful. But his delight is in the law of the Lord; and in His law doth he meditate both day and night. (Psalm 1:1–2)

Meditation was used by farmers of cows chewing their cud and of Roman senators reviewing their speeches before the speeches were delivered. Meditation is reviewing what the believer has learned. It is the secret to spiritual prosperity (Joshua 1:8). Paul wrote that believers should "give [themselves] wholly to meditation; that his profiting might appear to all" (1 Timothy 4:15). Meditation results in inner growth. It should accompany the other four methods of learning. This is why the thumb represents meditation. Meditation allows God's Word to transform the life of the believer.

Some like entertainment or sports. Others read the stock pages. If believers were as interested in God's Word as some people are interested in entertainment, sports schedules, or other reports, society would be a better place.

What Questions Should a Believer Ask When Studying God's Word?

Paul wrote, "Study to shew thyself approved unto God, a workman that needeth not to be ashamed, rightly dividing the Word of truth" (2 Timothy 2:15). Just as reporters ask journalistic questions of the events they cover, believers can ask questions of God's Word. These questions help the believer determine the meaning and proper application of God's Word to his life. Select a passage of scripture (Psalm 23 or some other passage) and ask the following questions of that passage. (Please look in the listings, at the end of this study, for this session's answers).

What was the author's intended m_____?

Every text has a purpose and a <u>meaning</u> intended by its author. No passage is of any "private interpretation" (2 Peter 1:21). God wants believers to understand His Word. Believers should seek to understand the mind-set of the author. In Psalm 23, the author wants the reader to appreciate the relationship of a compassionate shepherd with his sheep.

What is the immediate and wider c_____ of the passage?

How does the passage fit into the passages that surround it? The ultimate <u>context</u> is the entire Bible. The general context is the book in which the passage is found. The immediate context applies to the passages immediately before and immediately after the passage being studied. In Psalm 23, the context is the crucifixion of God's Lamb, as pictured in Psalm 22, and the sovereign reign of Jesus (in Psalm 24). Psalms 22–24 are a trio of chapters describing various aspects of Jesus Christ's death, ministry, and life.

What t_____ of passage is being studied?

The Bible includes a variety of literary <u>type</u>s. It includes history, prophecy, proverbs, parables, literal, narrative, allegorical, and other types of writings. Some passages have figures of speech. Other passages say, "This is that." The style and type of writing are important to an understanding of God's Word. Psalm 23 is one song in the hymnbook of Israel. It is described as "wisdom" literature and is a teaching passage.

What is the h_____, g_____, and c_____ context of the passage?

The Bible was not written in a vacuum. It was written in a context of <u>history</u>, <u>geography</u>, and <u>culture</u>. It is important to understand the text in the same way the original listener or reader understood the text. When reading a parable, see the truths as Christ's listeners would see those truths. When reading Psalm 23, it is important to interpret the psalm in the context of how a shepherd would understand the writing. Historically and geographically, Psalm 23 took place during the early life of David outside Bethlehem in the shepherd's fields, where a valley passes between two hills. Culturally, David was Jewish and was living in an agricultural (nonindustrial) society.

What is the g_____ s_____ of the passage (its hermeneutic)?

In looking at the grammatical structure of the passage, what are the subject, the verb, and the object? Is the subject a person or a thing? What is the tense and voice of the verb? Are there words which are associated with the subject, verb, and object (adjectives and adverbs)? In what way is the passage connected to previous passages and other passages in its context? How does the passage relate to the theme of the context? Good Bible students give attention to detail. Some Bible students diagram passages when they study God's Word. This allows the Bible student to see how each word is connected to the other words in the passage. In Psalm 23, highlights include the present tense of Psalm 23:1 (The Lord *is* my shepherd), the personal aspect of the relationship between the shepherd and the psalmist (knowing that the psalmist himself was a shepherd as well), and then the words and phrases of the psalm should be studied individually (in Psalm 23, describe the "green pastures" in a barren landscape; "stilled waters" are the only waters a sheep will drink; To "restore" is to turn around as in repentance; How does a shepherd lead: from ahead or from behind?; Ask: what is the identity and location of the valley?; What fears does the sheep experience? Who is with the psalmist?; What are the functions of the rod and the staff in relation to sheep?; Describe the table, the guests, and the anointing; What kind of traveling companions do goodness and mercy make?; and where is the psalmist now?) From the grammatical structure and its applications, an outline of the passage can be derived. Also, remember this: Often, the action verb (in the passage) leads the reader to the main thought. Many teaching outlines begin with the verbs.

What does the r_____ of the B_____ say about the passage being studies?

The extended context of every passage is the <u>rest</u> of the <u>Bible</u>. Believers should never read one passage of scripture in isolation from the remainder of the Bible. Believers should compare scripture with scripture. God is consistent in what He presents. Refuse to interpret scripture based on personal experiences. Interpret personal experiences based on the scripture. Allow the Bible to determine its own meaning. God's will never contradicts His revealed Word. God remains consistent with His Word.

Every time you study God's Word, "pray in" God's texts. Do more than pray for insight; pray that you can apply properly God's truths to your daily life. Prayer allows God to apply the texts to the daily life of believers.

What Are the Benefits of Studying God's Word?

In what ways does God's Word benefit the believer? Look up the following passages, match each passage to the corresponding truth, and if you have the companion workbook (*Spiritual Lessons for Growing Believers Workbook* published by WestBow Press), comment on the personal benefit you gain from studying God's Word in the spaces provided. (This is an in-exhaustive list. Please look in the listings, at the end of this study, to check your answers.)

Psalm 19:7–11   _____   A.   It brings new life (conversion) to the soul.

Psalm 119:9, 11   _____   B.   It builds up the believer in the faith.

Psalm 119:99   _____   C.   It helps the believer know and understand God's truth.

Psalm 119:105   _____   D.   It helps the believer know right from wrong.

Matthew 4:4   _____   E.   It keeps the believer from sin.

John 8:32   _____   F.   It gives direction and guidance to the believer's life.

John 17:17   _____   G.   It is spiritual bread (food) for the soul. (also 1 Peter 2:2; Hebrews 5:14.)

Acts 17:11   _____   H.   It makes the believer a better worker for God.

Acts 20:32   _____   I.   It reveals who God (Jesus) is.

Ephesians 3:19   _____   J.   It gives insight into what is fact and what is false.

2 Timothy 2:15   _____   K.   It liberates the believer.

Hebrews 5:14   _____   L.   It sanctifies believers (sets believers apart from sin).

The believer who wants to live a life consistent with God's character will study God's Word. Do it daily.

What Study Helps Are Available for Use in Studying God's Word?

A variety of study aids are available to help the believer study God's Word. They include the following. (This is an in-exhaustive list.)

> The Bible, resource materials from Christian bookstores and church libraries, Bible concordances, Bible dictionaries, Bible encyclopedias, Bible handbooks, Bible customs books, Bible maps, language helps, commentaries, additional reference books, theology books, hymnbooks, worship guides, seminars, workshops, conferences, Bible study manuals, electronic media, fellowship groups, Bible studies, language helps, internet and website materials, and other resources and aids.

Believers can study God's Word anytime and anywhere. Believers can study a word, a phrase, a sentence, a verse, a chapter, or a book. Bible study can be private, with the family before or after a meal, or with a group. When studying the Bible, read it through (get something specific), pray it in (apply it), write it down (mark your Bible or keep a notebook), work it out (in daily life), and pass it on (tell others). Be creative and be consistent with the content of God's Word.

Of the Bible, an author wrote,

> This book contains the mind of God, the state of man, the way of salvation, the doom of sinners,

and the happiness of believers ... Read it to be wise, believe it to be safe, and practice it to be holy ... It is the traveler's map, the pilgrim's staff, the pilot's compass, the soldier's sword, and the Christian's charter. Here Paradise is restored, heaven opened, and the gates of hell disclosed. Christ is the grand subject, our good its design, and the glory of God its end ... Read it slowly, frequently, and prayerfully ... It is given to you in life, will be opened at the judgment ... will reward the greatest labor, and condemns all who trifle with its sacred contents.[14]

Get everything you can from God's Word. A study of the Bible will bless your life.

For your encouragement, participate in the following exercises:

1. Conduct Bible studies in the following passage types:

    -   allegorical/prophecy (Matthew 24–25)
    -   narrative (1 Samuel 17)
    -   literal/expository (Ephesians 1:3–14)

2. Compare scripture with scripture on the following topics:

    -   marriage (Genesis 1:21–25; 2:20; Ephesians 5:21–33)

---

14 Priscilla Howe's "The Bible," as quoted in *Uncle Ben's Quotebook* (Grand Rapids, MI: Baker Book House, 1976), 57.

- the home (Deuteronomy 6:4–9; Proverbs 22:6; Ephesians 6:1–4)
- a salvation relationship of grace compared to a religion of works (Galatians)

3. Conduct some personal Bible studies by applying the information provided in this study.

Study 1: What God Does with Sin

- Psalm 32:1
- Psalm 32:2
- Psalm 103:12
- Isaiah 1:18
- Isaiah 38:17
- Isaiah 43:25
- Isaiah 55:7
- Micah 7:19
- Matthew 26:28
- John 1:29
- Hebrews 1:3
- 1 John 1:9

Study 2: Bible Be's

- Be_____   Job 22:21
- Be_____   Joshua 1:6
- Be_____   Matthew 5:48
- Be_____   Matthew 14:27
- Be_____   Ephesians 4:32
- Be_____   James 5:7
- Be_____   1 Peter 5:5
- Be_____   1 Peter 5:5
- Be_____   1 Peter 5:8
- Be_____   2 Peter 3:14

Study 3: Some Sure Things

- Thou shalt surely _____.   Genesis 2:17
- Be sure your _____ will find you out.   Numbers 32:23
- The _____ of God standeth sure.   2 Timothy 2:19
- The sure word of the _____ of God.   2 Peter 1:19
- Surely I _____ quickly.   Revelation 22:20

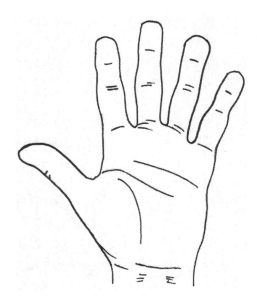

The following are five methods believers can use to learn from the scriptures. (Use the key terms in this section to complete the hand illustration.[15])

- Romans 10:17 _____ the Word.
- Revelation 1:3 _____ the Word.
- Acts 17:11 _____ the Word.
- Psalm 119:9, 11) _____ the Word.
- Psalm 1:1–2 _____ on God's Word.

15 The drawing of the prayer hand is used by permission of the artist Beth S. Pisani.

Answers to the "How to Study the Bible" Session
(For the Discipler)

Why Should Believers Have a Quiet Time of Study/ Devotion with God?

Joshua 1:6–8	Meditation
Psalm 119:9, 11	Sin
Psalm 119:105, 130	Light
Proverbs 2:1–5	Wisdom
Jeremiah 15:16	Joy
Acts 17:10–14	Stability
1 Peter 2:2	Growth
2 Timothy 2:15	Obey/Study

What Should Believers Include When Having a Quiet Time of Study/Devotion with God?

Hand Illustration

Romans 10:17	<u>Hear</u> the Word.
Revelation 1:3	<u>Read</u> the Word.
Acts 17:11	<u>Study</u> the Word.
Psalm 119:9, 11	<u>Memorize</u> the Word.
Psalm 1:1–2	<u>Meditate</u> on God's Word.

What Questions Should a Believer Ask When Studying God's Word?

What was the author's intended <u>meaning</u>?
What is the immediate and wider <u>context</u> of the passage?
What <u>type</u> of passage is being studied?
What is the <u>historical</u>, <u>geographical</u>, and <u>cultural</u> context of the passage?
What is the <u>grammatical structure</u> of the passage (its hermeneutic)?
What does the <u>rest</u> of the <u>Bible</u> say about the passage being studied?

What Are the Benefits of Studying God's Word?

In what ways does God's Word benefit the believer? Look up the following passages, match each passage to the corresponding truth, and if you have the companion workbook, comment on the personal benefit you gain from studying God's Word in the spaces provided. (This is an in-exhaustive list.)

Psalm 19:7–11	_A_	A.	It brings new life (conversion) to the soul.
Psalm 119:9, 11	_E_	B.	It builds up the believer in the faith.
Psalm 119:99	_C_	C.	It helps the believer know and understand God's truth.
Psalm 119:105	_F_	D.	It helps the believer know right from wrong.
Matthew 4:4	_G_	E.	It keeps the believer from sin.
John 8:32	_K_	F.	It gives direction and guidance to the believer's life.
John 17:17	_L_	G.	It is spiritual bread (food) for the soul. (also 1 Peter 2:2; Hebrews 5:14.)
Acts 17:11	_J_	H.	It makes the believer a better worker for God.
Acts 20:32	_B_	I.	It reveals who God (Jesus) is.

Ephesians 3:19 ___I___ J. It gives insight into what is fact and what is false.

2 Timothy 2:15 ___H___ K. It liberates the believer.

Hebrews 5:14 ___D___ L. It sanctifies believers (sets believers apart).

What Bible Study Helps Are Available for Use in Studying God's Word?

The Bible, resource materials from Christian bookstores and church libraries, Bible concordances, Bible dictionaries, Bible encyclopedias, Bible handbooks, Bible customs books, Bible maps, language helps, commentaries, additional reference books, theology books, hymnbooks, worship guides, seminars, workshops, conferences, Bible study manuals, electronic media, fellowship groups, Bible studies, language helps, internet and website materials, and other resources and aids.

Exercises

1. Conduct Bible studies in the following passage types:

    ○ allegorical/prophecy (Matthew 24–25)—Christ's Olivet Discourse

    ○ narrative (1 Samuel 17)—David and Goliath

- literal/expository (Ephesians 1:3–14)—Paul's doctrinal teachings

2. Compare scripture with scripture on the following topics:

   - marriage (Genesis 1:21–25; 2:20; Ephesians 5:21–33)

   - the home (Deuteronomy 6:4–9; Proverbs 22:6; Ephesians 6:1–4)

   - a salvation relationship of grace compared to a religion of works (Galatians)

3. Conduct some personal Bible studies by applying the information provided in this study.

Study 1: What God Does with Sin

Psalm 32:1	God forgives/covers our sins.
Psalm 32:2	God does not impute iniquity. (God does not hold our sins against us).
Psalm 103:12	God removes our transgressions as far as the east is from the west.
Isaiah 1:18	Our sins are changed from scarlet to as white as snow.

Isaiah 38:17	God casts our sins behind His back where He "cannot" see them.
Isaiah 43:25	God blots out our sins and remembers them no more.
Isaiah 55:7	God has mercy and abundantly pardons.
Micah 7:19	God casts our sins into the depths of the sea.
Matthew 26:28	God remits our sins. (He forgives our sins.)
John 1:29	God takes away the sins of the world.
Hebrews 1:3	God purges our sins/purifies us from sins.
1 John 1:9	God cleanses us from sin.

Study 2: Bible Be's

Be at peace.	Job 22:21
Be strong/courageous.	Joshua 1:6
Be perfect/spiritually mature.	Matthew 5:48

Be <u>of good cheer.</u>	Matthew 14:27
Be <u>kind.</u>	Ephesians 4:32
Be <u>patient.</u>	James 5:7
Be <u>submissive/under authority.</u>	1 Peter 5:5
Be <u>humble.</u>	1 Peter 5:5
Be <u>sober/serious about God and vigilant.</u>	1 Peter 5:8
Be <u>diligent/spiritually aware.</u>	2 Peter 3:14

Study 3: Some Sure Things

Thou shalt surely <u>die</u>.	Genesis 2:17
Be sure your <u>sins</u> will find you out.	Numbers 32:23
The <u>foundation</u> of God standeth sure.	2 Timothy 2:19
The sure word of the <u>prophecy/revelation</u> of God.	2 Peter 1:19
Surely I <u>come</u> quickly.	Revelation 22:20

Selected Bibliography

Arnt, William and Gingrech, F. William. *A Greek-English Lexicon of the New Testament*. London: The University of Chicago Press, 1957. S.v. *"bapto,"* 132.

Dejong, Benjamin R. *Uncle Ben's Quotebook*. Grand Rapids, MI: Baker Book House, 1976.

Doan, Eleanor. *Speaker's Sourcebook*. Grand Rapids, MI: Zondervan, 1960.

The Holy Bible, the King James Version.

Liddell, Henry George and Scott, Robert. *A Greek-English Lexicon*. London: Oxford University Press, 1996. S.v. *"bapto,"* 305.

Pisani, Keith D. *Spiritual Lessons for Growing Believers*. Nashville, TN: WestBow Press, 2016.

Thayer, Joseph Henry. *Thayer's Greek-English Lexicon of the New Testament*. Grand Rapids, MI: Zondervan, 1962. S.v. *"bapto,"* 95.